MIDDI

DURING THE
GREAT DEPRESSION

By

MARY ANN LABUTTA

Edited by
Donald K. Miller and
Paul T. Miller

2006

To order additional copies, please contact us.
BookSurge, LLC
www.booksurge.com
1-866-308-6235
orders@booksurge.com

CONTENTS

FOREWORD

These pages are meant to preserve an account of middle class life in the 1930's and into the 1940's. It would have been easier if this was written before I was declared legally blind. It is difficult without the feedback of seeing what is already written.

These memories come from the perspective of someone who lived in a rural area of southwestern Pennsylvania. This rural area was surrounded by many small towns within a radius of about 5 miles (each averaging about 1000 residents). Ninety percent of the homes in these small towns were owned by large companies. The large companies also owned the coal mines and the company stores. These homes were sold to families during the 1940's——after the depression years.

One of my duties when I worked in a company store, was to visit customers' homes regularly and take orders for any items they wanted delivered. Knowing the people and visiting their homes over a period of several years, gives me an overall knowledge of how the middle class lived.

1
Everyday Living

During the depression years (the 1930's) there was little or no communication and practically no health care. The homes, work place, and life, in general, were all so different than they are today.

Only the bare necessities were bought, because there was no extra money for even the smallest purchase. My father was one of the fortunate ones, in that, he always had a job in the coal mine——but for several years, he worked 3 days in two weeks ($5.00 a day). Yet, my parents were able to support a family of six children, and we never thought of ourselves as poor.

Sometime in the mid 1930's, my older sister and older brother found jobs, and that helped my parents with supporting the family. One of the decisions my parents made was to 'cash in' life insurance policies, to help them through the most difficult times.

Vegetable gardens and home canning were a common thing in most households. Canning jars came in pint, quart, and half gallon sizes. Vegetables and fruits were put into jars (that had been sterilized), covered with either salted or sugared water and sealed with a threaded top. Then, these filled jars were boiled in a large water bath. Some things that we had in canning jars were: tomatoes, green beans, corn, meat, pickles, piccalilli (a mixture of sliced cucumbers, green peppers, onions and green tomatoes), peaches, pears, cherries, and all kinds of jams and jellies made from fruits and berries picked in the fields and in the woods.

Many families kept chickens in the backyards, and pigs in an area beyond the yards. Chickens provided eggs for the family, and were later used to provide meat for meals.

Pigs were always slaughtered when the weather turned cold, and the men would help one another in this effort. They would cut the carcasses into cooking and roasting sizes the family desired. Hams and ribs were smoked and cured in homemade smokehouses (shared by several families). Sausage was made using a crude machine to form the shapes. Some of the meat was cooked, cut into pieces, and preserved in canning jars. Sometimes the cooked meat was put into a large earthenware container (called a crock) and covered with lard (animal fat). Can you imagine using animal fat in this way? The meat that was smoked and cured was kept in an unheated room, or even outdoors if it could be protected from the animals. All these things had to be done because there was no refrigeration.

Potatoes, onions, carrots, and fruits were stored in the coolest spot——most often below ground level in a fruit cellar. Cabbage was sometimes shredded, salted, and put into a crock to ferment until it became sauerkraut.

Bread was baked 2 or 3 times a week. Some families had large, outdoor brick ovens for just this purpose. Sliced, wrapped bread from a store was considered a real treat!

Most meals were made using some variety of dough, potatoes, onions, cabbage, dried beans and any available vegetable. A variety of soups were cooked 2 or 3 times a week, adding homemade noodles or dumplings. We probably had meat for the main meal 3 or 4 times a week. Cakes and pies were baked 2 or 3 times a week, and cookies were baked only for the holidays.

On Saturdays (in high school gymnasiums) the government distributed 25# flour, 10# sugar, rice, and cheese to those who were unemployed. The flour came in printed cloth bags. When empty, these bags were ripped open, washed and bleached, then used as needed by each household. Most often they were used to make dish towels, aprons, or pillowcases.

Many of the young men (17-20 years of age) were recruited in a government program meant to provide financial help for families. These young men joined the Civilian Conservation Corps (CCC Camps) and worked to check soil erosion, reforestation and flood control. They earned $30 a month. The government sent $25 to the parents and the young men received $5 plus meals and a place to live.

The Works Progress Administration (WPA) was created in the mid 1930's. The WPA was a government program intended to alleviate some of the most difficult unemployment problems. Men were employed to build roads, bridges, parks, tunnels, buildings, walls along waterways and other construction projects. Women were employed to rebind and redo used books. Those men and women were paid a minimum amount that helped the families to survive.

MARY ANN LABUTTA

2

Economics

P rices were comparable to what men were earning. Bread cost 5 cents for a 16 oz. loaf, and milk cost 10 cents a quart. Milk was sold only in glass quart bottles that had a paper lid and a paper covering. A whole pork loin cost 70—80 cents——7 cents a pound. The price of gasoline was 16.9 cents a gallon everywhere, and the price never changed over a period of 15—20 years.

Workers did not receive a pay check—they received a pay envelope. Cash was put into a special kind of envelope, with the earnings calculated on the outside. There were no deductions, because no one earned enough to pay income tax. Then, in 1936 came the first deductions for Social Security.

Checks were not used because the middle class had no reason to use banks. Everything was paid for with cash——rents, utility bills (if any), grocery bills, and any charge accounts. Credit cards were unheard of. These charge accounts had to be paid in full every month or two——or the credit was discontinued. Car insurance, house insurance and medical insurance were unheard of, very unlike the expenses families have today.

Several years ago, we found tax receipts in my parents' home. These receipts show that the annual property tax my parents paid was $2.34 for a 4—room house on 5 acres of land. In those days a tax collector came door-to-door collecting taxes.

MARY ANN LABUTTA

Another fact to mention: My husband earned a Bachelor of Science Degree between 1937—1941 at a total cost of $628.00 for tuition and books.

3
Homes and Fashions

A major factor about homes in the 1930's was that so few had central heating, electricity, or running water. There were heating stoves that burned coal and wood, and oil lamps were used in every room. When a house had no running water, water was hand-pumped from deep wells or collected from natural springs, then carried to the homes. It was common to see rain barrels at the corners of a house. Water came from the roofs, through the drainpipes and collected in these barrels. This water was used for everything except drinking and cooking.

The furniture in a middle class home was very simple and basic. A table and chairs, a stove, a sink, a freestanding cabinet (or two) about 7 ft. high, and an icebox made up the kitchen. Oilcloth, sold by the yard, was used to cover the kitchen table. This oilcloth was kept clean by wiping with soap and water. The cabinet, or cabinets, were used to store dishes, cups, glasses, silverware, pots, pans, linens, towels, any medical aids and toothbrushes.

The icebox was a wooden cabinet about 3 ft. high by 3 ft. wide, insulated as best known at the time. The family would place a card in the front window indicating the size block of ice the iceman was to deliver. The top shelf of the icebox had space enough for a few items, (such as milk and meat) that needed to be kept cool. There was a deep pan at the bottom of the icebox. This pan had to be emptied as the block of ice melted. Refrigerators were not manufactured for household use until about the mid 1930's. The kitchen floor was most often covered with a 9 ft. X 12 ft. congoleum rug, with painted floors along the sides. Some homes had an unfinished wooden floor in the kitchen.

The bedrooms were just as simple and basic. Most beds were iron-framed, and this is a time before innerspring mattresses. How mattresses were constructed is unknown to me. The mattresses were laid on top of bedsprings that were open and uncovered. Bedroom closets, if any, were 2 ft. X 4 ft., and they were unimportant because people had very little clothing. There might be a freestanding wooden cabinet (called a chifferobe or armoire) in which a few clothes could be hung on hangers, and some storage space in a few drawers. Adult's and children's shoes were kept lined up in pairs under the beds.

Many households had a treadle sewing machine. A treadle was a pedal moved by flexing the foot. The treadle was connected to a large wheel by a rubber belt, and that mechanically moved a needle to do the stitching.

Treadle sewing machine

Living room furniture was mostly wood-framed on the backs and on the side arms, with the back and the seat slightly cushioned. Only a few families had over-stuffed furniture in the living room. Woven rugs (9 ft. X 12 ft.) usually covered the floor with painted floors along the four sides. The radio was the focal point in the living room, most often a console. A console means that the radio with all its parts was enclosed in a wooden cabinet probably 30 inches high X 20 inches wide. There were only a few radio stations, and reception of radio signals depended so much on atmospheric conditions. This was so noticeable when a storm was approaching——the cracking sounds (static) were so loud, it was best to turn off the radio.

If there was a dining room, the dining room table was

covered with a hand-embroidered tablecloth, a lace tablecloth or a tablecloth that had been hand-crocheted.

My mother had one of the first washing machines——a Maytag (with a wringer) that was operated by a gasoline motor. A wringer was made up of two hard rubber rollers about 12 inches long that squeezed the water from the clothes during the washing process.

Clothes had to be lifted from the hot wash water with a 'washer stick', put through the wringer into the rinse water. Then, lifted from the rinse water, put through the wringer again, and into a basket of the finished clothes. Today we have plastic baskets, but at that time, bushel baskets (from fruits and vegetables) were lined with newspaper or cloth and used for the laundry.

During the summer months (with the basement door open), you could be 100 ft. away and hear the putt-putt of the gasoline motor that powered the washing machine. Nearby children would be drawn by the sound and come to watch my mother do the laundry.

There were no hot water heaters. Water had to be heated on a stove in a large copper container (called a boiler), and then dumped into the washing machine with soap powder. Hot water had to be used to dissolve the soap, because detergents were non-existent. The same water was used over and over again to wash and rinse 8—10 loads of clothes. You had to be careful to wash the clothes in the proper order: white shirts and blouses, sheets (all sheets were white), underwear and pajamas, towels, light colored clothing, dark colored clothing, work clothes, and finally, the throw rugs.

Throw rugs were used in every room. These throw rugs were made from worn out clothing, sheets, etc. that were cut into 1—inch strips, sewn together, and rolled into large balls. These balls were passed from one side to the other through a loom, and beat into a tight pattern to make rugs that measured about 20 inches wide by any desired length. Some families made these rugs to sell to those who needed more rugs.

After the clothes had been washed, everything had to be hung to dry. This was no easy task on rainy days or during the winter months. On these days, most often the clothes were hung indoors on clotheslines that were strung across the rooms just below the ceilings. Can you imagine what it was like to walk into a house, with wet clothes hanging on these clotheslines?

Because of the quality of materials, everything had to be ironed——even the sheets and underwear. There were no steam irons, so the dried clothes were dampened before ironing, to remove the wrinkles. Doing the washing and ironing would take about 3 days with no interruptions.

Just about every house was thoroughly cleaned at least once a year. As a result of coal heat, the walls, woodwork, windows, curtains, furniture, and rugs were very soiled. Most homes had woven 9 ft. X 12 ft. rugs in special rooms. To remove the dirt, these woven rugs were rolled up, carried outdoors and hung over a clothesline. They were then beat from both sides with a carpet beater. The carpet beater was slightly larger than a tennis racket——made from wires in a certain design, with a wooden handle. There were no vacuum cleaners——only a long-handled carpet sweeper that moved a brush over the rugs. The brush pushed the surface dirt into a compartment that was then emptied.

Women and girls never wore pants. They only wore dresses and skirts. Even on the coldest days, our legs were covered only with cotton stockings, unless you wore long underwear. It was an embarrassment for females to wear long underwear when you were teenage or older. As adults, women seldom wore silk stockings, because of the high cost and the tendency to get 'runners'.

A new product, nylon was first used for parachutes during World War II. When the war ended in 1945, then, nylon was used to make women's stockings. The cotton stockings, the silk stockings, and the nylon stockings were all made to be held up with garters or a garter belt. The garters were sometimes made with elastic sold by the yard. Women and girls always wore hats to church, and anytime they were dressed to go somewhere special (even shopping).

Men's stockings were different, too. They were held up with supporters that were snapped on just below the knees. The sleeves on men's dress shirts were all one length———so men wore a garter just above the elbow to raise the sleeve to the right length. Men wore hats most of the time. There were clips in the church pews especially for hanging men's hats. Young boys wore 'high-top' shoes, with a pocket on the outside of one shoe to carry a pocket knife.

4

Unusual Facts

During the depression years, teenage boys (13-17 years of age) would sometimes leave home just to make it easier for the family to survive, with 'one less mouth to feed'. They would 'ride the rails', hopping on trains, going from place to place, and working at any odd job they could find. In the small town where I attended elementary school, there were two young men who had one leg amputated as a result of hopping on trains.

Some of these facts about the earlier years will surprise the younger generations.

When a person died, a funeral director came to take the body to be embalmed. Because there were so few cars, and friends and family could not go to a funeral home, wakes were held in the homes of the deceased.

All the furniture in the livingroom was moved to another part of the house—and sometimes even to a neighbor's house. The funeral director brought the body in a casket, to the livingroom along with the folding chairs for anyone attending the wake.

It was the custom that someone had to stay awake all night in the home. So, men came together (usually 3 or 4) and volunteered for this service. Most often they played cards to help them stay awake until morning.

Wakes went on for 2 or 3 days and nights, with no specific

visiting hours. People came anytime to pay their respects, because someone was always in the house. Families and friends provided the food, pastries and drinks for those who came to the wake.

My parents had a cistern that gave us our water supply. It was a brick-walled storage tank built below ground level. Water was collected from the roof of the house during a rainfall. When it started to rain, we had to wait until the roof had been washed and the water ran clear, before it could be channeled into the cistern. The water was then filtered and pumped into the house by an electric pump that was in the basement. If the summer was dry, the water level of the cistern would go down, and the volunteer fire department (from one of the small towns) would bring their tank truck, and fill the cistern to last until needed again.

My father and two older brothers would pick mushrooms in our field at certain times of the year. We all enjoyed fried mushrooms and were glad when they brought in enough to fill 2 large frying pans. By the time the mushrooms were finished frying, there was only enough to fill a serving bowl. A fungus grew around the base of several poplar trees that lined the front of our property. People going by would ask permission to fill their containers with these fungi, which were prepared in the same way as mushrooms.

My father had a horseradish plant in the backyard. When he would grind the horseradish root to prepare with vinegar, the fumes filled the house and burned the eyes, nose and throat. We all hated that day!

Just about every household had a 'last', because most fathers were amateur cobblers who resoled and reheeled the family shoes. A 'last' is an iron stand about 24 inches high, with an iron insole at the top of the stand. The shoe to be repaired was slipped over the iron insole, with the bottom of the shoe facing upward, in a position to be repaired. To save the money needed to purchase leather for the resoles, sometimes worn-out leather miner's belts (2 ½—3 inches wide) were cut in pieces and used to resole shoes.

Shoe 'last'

Imagine a time when there were very few cars, and people could seldom go shopping. Enterprising men would bring their products, and go door-to-door in the small towns and through the countryside. The man who sold fruits and vegetables from the back of a truck was called a huckster. Another man brought bolts of fabric and other items needed for dressmaking. He also sold sheets, towels, blankets, bedspreads, and curtains. This man, called a peddler, would take orders for anything the family wanted to buy on his next sales trip. One man sold doughnuts and ladylocks (a creme-filled pastry) from the back seat of his car. A photographer would visit once a year, especially taking pictures of the very young children. Occasionally, he brought a pony for just this reason. Farmers sold milk to regular customers, and this milk was never pasteurized!

During these years, many beggars were visible——mostly men whose legs had been amputated as a result of a mine accident, or they were otherwise disabled. There was no government aid, and people gave of their meager means to help the less fortunate. Most of these men asked only for something to eat and just a few pennies.

One of the ways teenagers could earn a little money was picking berries for nearby farmers. They were paid 1 cent for a quart, and the berries were sold for 8-10 cents a quart. The only source of income for the small farmers was selling milk and eggs, until the harvest season when they sold berries, fruits and vegetables.

Young men and women only moved from the parent's house if they were relocating to a completely different area because of a job. They lived with the parents until they decided to marry. Sometimes the newly married couple lived with the parents a few years, because of poor financial conditions.

An unusual historical fact is that President Franklin D. Roosevelt was the only president to serve more than 8 years. He was inaugurated in early 1933, and died while in office in April of 1945. To make sure that does not happen again, the 22nd Amendment to the Constitution now limits a president to 2 elective terms.

5

Schools

Schools in the 1920's and 1930's were so unlike what they became in later years. Each small town had its own elementary school. The buildings were very simple——just the large classrooms, with no other room or office. The 8th grade teacher was the principal with no supervisory responsibility. His main job as principal was to discipline unruly students.

There were no lockers. There was a narrow 'cloak room' along one side of each classroom, where the students hung their coats and kept their lunches. The elementary school buildings had no central heating. Each classroom was heated by a large coal-burning furnace, and you had to wonder how the students on the opposite side of the room kept warm. The older boys had the duties to carry coal from the 'coal house' to the classrooms to keep the furnace fire burning. They used coal buckets that probably held 25-30 pounds of coal. The boys also removed the ashes when needed.

The elementary school buildings had electricity but no running water (indoor plumbing), and that had to have contributed to the many contagious diseases. We didn't even have a drinking fountain. There was an enameled bucket of drinking water in the front of the classroom, and everyone drank water from the same long-handled dipper.

Cleaning the classroom in the elementary schools was the

responsibility of each teacher. The teachers had to hire and also pay their own janitor. My brother-in-law was the janitor for a couple of teachers. He washed the blackboards, dusted the erasers, and swept the floor at the end of each school day. For this work, he was paid $2.00 a month (10 cents a day) for each classroom. During the cold months, the janitor would also remove the ashes from the furnace, and cover the furnace fire with fine coal, so that the fire would just simmer for the entire night. In the morning, the teacher would stir and start the fire burning again.

There were no personal contacts between the teachers and the parents. In those days, there were no home telephones and the parents were not invited to the schools. The teachers were in complete charge of disciplining the students during the school day. Most often, the teachers used small wooden paddles to punish the students.

Subjects taught the first 4 years were: reading, writing, arithmetic and spelling. The only subjects added in the 5th grade were: history, geography, English and health, and those studies continued four full years.

Good penmanship was always emphasized. Cursive writing was a part of every school day. Starting in the 5th grade, the desk tops had a hole for an ink well (liquid blue ink). We used wooden pen holders with disposable pen points that were dipped in the ink before writing. Blotters (sponge-like papers (3 in. x 6 in.)) were used to soak up the ink usually left on the surface of the paper.

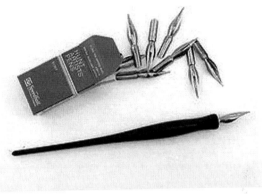

Pen holder with disposable pen point

In high school, we were introduced to a variety of studies. Here, the buildings had central heating, water fountains and lavatories.

MARY ANN LABUTTA

6

Homemade Beverages

The 18th Amendment to the Constitution made it unlawful to buy or sell alcoholic beverages, until it was repealed in the mid 1930's. This period of about 15 years is called Prohibition.

Many families made their own beer—called 'home brew'. The grocery stores sold a large can of malt (a derivative of barley) that was mixed with yeast and water in a large crock, then, set aside to ferment until it became beer. This process finished, the beer was siphoned into quart bottles, and a glass top was put in place with a spring—like closure. Many backyards had a grape arbor and wine was made from some of these grapes. Wine was also made from the many varieties of berries that grew in the fields and in the woods.

There were a few 'bootleggers' living in most of the small towns. The bootleggers were men who made distilled liquor (moonshine) in their homes or somewhere near their homes. They sold the liquor secretly only to friends they could trust. The bootleggers trusted their friends would not tell the authorities where they had purchased the liquor. If the men were arrested for selling liquor, they usually had to serve time in jail.

Some families made root beer, following the directions on a small bottle of root beer extract. This soft drink was siphoned into pop bottles and catsup bottles that had been saved for just this purpose. The filled glass bottles were closed with a hand-driven 'capper', that closed down tightly on a metal cap. They were set aside to 'ripen' in a warm place covered with a blanket. A few bottles would always explode.

This is a time to mention that all beverages were sold in bottles. They were sold with a paid deposit, and the bottles were returned when making another purchase. Cans were not used for beverages until probably the 1960's.

7

Diseases and Health Care

During the 1920's and the 1930's, most homes had no indoor plumbing and that was a factor contributing to the many contagious diseases. Very few homes had a bathroom——instead, there were outside toilets. There were no facilities to wash the hands near the toilets. Things were not sanitary as they are today, and that was a cause of poorer health and a shorter life span.

When a family was hit by a contagious disease, a sign was put on the front of the house designating the disease, and it stated that the family was quarantined. No one was permitted to enter or leave the house except the head of the household. How much do we hear today about whooping cough, scarlet fever, mumps, measles, small pox, typhoid fever, diphtheria, or tuberculosis?

Health care was almost non-existent. Families used all kinds of home remedies to treat both young and old. The only available painkillers were Bayer aspirin and anacin. Most doctors were in general medicine and made house calls—— even delivering babies. The doctor's office and waiting room always occupied the front rooms of his home—with his 'shingle' displayed somewhere in front of his home. A shingle was a small signboard on which the doctor's name was engraved.

Visiting a doctor was so different, in that, there were no appointments (no telephones). You went to a doctor's waiting room and waited for your turn. There was no preventive medicine. People only visited a doctor if there had been a home accident, an unusually high fever, or for a serious ailment for which an operation may be needed. When an operation was needed, the family doctor made all the arrangements with a surgeon.

Eye care was so uncommon. There were a few opticians, but most often people would go to Sears Roebuck or a 5 & 10 cents store (Woolworths or Kresges), try on glasses that best suited them for reading, and bought that pair. Few people ever went to a dentist, and most often only in an emergency. I remember that a friend's father died because he had no treatment for an abscessed tooth!

8

Family Travel

Our family made trips every year to visit extended family in Detroit. These trips must have taken many hours from southwestern Pennsylvania. All national and state routes were 2-lane and cars were not made to travel the speeds they do today. We had to travel through all the small towns and cities, many traffic lights, and were stopped at the many railroad crossings. There were no restrictions nor a time limit on how long a train could have the traffic stopped at these crossings.

We never stopped at the few restaurants along the way. Instead, we packed egg salad and meat sandwiches for the stops along the roadside. There were no coolers, and we had no idea it was unsafe to eat those sandwiches!

Two cars that my father drove during these years were the Elgin and the Chandler. The Chandler had two chair-like jump seats that were pulled up and put into place between the front seat and the back seat. There were always 7 or 8 of us in the car, and seat belts were unheard of at the time.

One of the sights along the highways kept us alert and watchful. Those were the 4 or 5 Burma Shave signs, spaced about 10 feet apart that always gave a positive message in rhyming lines. We probably read these different messages several times on these trips to and from Detroit. What a time for family travel.

MARY ANN LABUTTA

9
Games and Entertainment

Children found ways to play outdoors without the use of any equipment. Hide and seek, kick the can, and catchers (tag) were all so common. A game was called 'caddy', in which a 4-sided, 6-inch long wooden piece (whittled) was hit with a paddle, to see who could hit it the farthest. The high score depended on how the whittled piece landed. It had to land with the IV side facing upward to get the highest score. A game was played using a pocket knife, testing who could go through all the positions, and have the pocket knife stick upright in the ground from each position. This game was only played after a rainfall when the ground was soft.

Children would step on empty cans until the cans wrapped around the shoes——then, they would walk and run on them. Homemade stilts were a common sight, so teenagers became adept at using them. My two older brothers built 4 hurdles in the lower backyard. They would run and jump these hurdles, and the loser had to do the next family chore. Horseshoes were used a lot by older children and adults——especially when several were gathered and they could play in teams.

The only toys available for children were: wagons, sleds, teddy bears, dolls, kiddie carts, crayons and coloring books, yoyos, marbles, a few wooden toys, a few wind-up toys, and wind-up trains. These toys lasted many years, handed down to younger children.

There were so many card games, and we spent many evenings playing cards until the late hours. Some of the card games were: Rummy, Pinochle, 500, Hearts, 31, Crazy 8's, and George. Jigsaw puzzles were very popular and were traded 'back and forth' with other families. Just about every household had a checkerboard with checkers and a set of dominoes.

Admission to a movie cost ten cents, and the price was raised a little with the introduction of color to the big screen. One of the first color movies was "Trail of the Lonesome Pine" in about 1937. Who could go to the movies when there were so few cars, and only some of the small cities had streetcars?

Dances were held on the weekends in church halls, high school gymnasiums, and a few dance halls. There was only 'live music' played by two, three, or four musicians, who played popular dance music, country music and polkas. Admission was 25-50 cents and was limited to those over the age of sixteen.

An open-air dance hall (called 'Smilin' Thru') was located about a mile from our home. This dance hall had just a roof overhead and a closed banister along the sides. Young people, in groups, would walk from as far away as three miles to attend these dances. You could stand outside the banister, listen to the music and watch the dancers——only had to pay admission to enter the hall. This is where so many learned to dance to different kinds of music.

The Ivory Ballroom in Uniontown was a special dance hall, having larger bands for the evenings entertainment. At every dance, in every dance hall, the last song of the evening was always "Stardust". The musicians would play the first bars of "Stardust", and the male dancers would choose their partners for the final dance of the evening. This is the time that is known as the 'big band era'

Big Band Era

Guy Lombardo	Glenn Miller
Tommy Dorsey	Benny Goodman
Sammy Kaye	Jimmy Dorsey
Harry James	Wayne King
Artie Shaw	Les Brown
Gene Krupa	

We listened to big band music on phonograph records (72 rpm) and on the radio. During the depression years, some of the comedians on radio were:

Comedians

Amos n' Andy	Joe Penner
Fibber McGee and Molly	Jack Benny
George Burns and Gracie Ellen	Edgar Bergen and Charlie McCarthy

MARY ANN LABUTTA

10
The Work Place

Our country was recovering from the depression in 1940. That year I started to work as a bookkeeper/cashier in a 'company store' owned by U.S. Steel Company. This was a department store that sold: food, clothing, shoes, hardware, jewelry, house wares, bedding, linens, furniture, appliances, tires, and gasoline. There was no such thing as overtime pay——8 hours a day, 6 days a week, until all the work was finished each day. This averaged 50-55 hours a week, so that earning $15.00 a week meant I was paid less than 30 cents an hour. Yet, I was fortunate to have that job. With the coming of 'Unionism', the salaries increased over the next several years.

Very few people had cars, and telephones for home use were even less common. The stores had delivery trucks, and this delivery service was used by most families. One of my assigned duties was to visit customers' homes one day every 2 weeks, and take orders for items they wanted delivered in a few days. Common items ordered were: 25# flour, 10# sugar, 30# potatoes, canned vegetables, a few cereals, rice, dried beans, crackers, a few bars of soap, soap powder, cheese, butter and eggs. Very few families bought paper products. Instead of toilet tissue, they used the sheets from the Sears Roebuck and Montgomery Ward catalogs. Those catalogs were hanging on a nail in the outside toilets. Handkerchiefs were used instead of

Kleenex. Probably 10 percent of the customers ordered feed for the chickens, pigs, and a few cattle that were kept somewhere near their homes.

It would be difficult to imagine how few products were available in comparison to what we have today. The only shortenings were lard, margarine and butter. There was a law in many states to encourage the sale and purchase of butter. Because of this law, margarine could not look like butter. Margarine had to be white, and was sold with a coloring tablet, that was mixed in at home to make the margarine yellow.

There were only a few cereals: corn flakes, wheaties, shredded wheat, all-bran, puffed rice and puffed wheat. There were about 6 different bars of hand soaps and soap powders were few.

Cookies were not sold in bags or boxes. Grocery stores had a special kind of stand, where cookies were displayed in large boxes shaped like 12-inch cubes. These boxes probably held 10-12 pounds of cookies. When put on display, the top of a box was replaced with an isinglass (mica) see-through lid. The clerk would put the desired amount of cookies into a brown bag (there was no plastic) then weigh the cookies. In these boxes were some of the same cookies we have today: vanilla wafers, fig newtons, sugar cookies, oreos, sandwich cookies, macaroons, oatmeal cookies, marshmallow cookies, ginger snaps and a few others.

Purchases in stores were handled very differently in those days. There was no self-serve——customers could not pick out the items they wanted to buy. Everything was displayed on shelves along the walls behind the long counters where customers stood, or was displayed in closed showcases. The only things the customers could pick out were the few fresh fruits and vegetables.

The clerk behind the counter collected all the items together, wrote the items on a receipt (with carbon paper between two sheets), and carried out the price to the money column where it was mentally totaled. There were no calculators. There was a crude adding machine for office use only. This adding machine was hand operated——a handle was pulled after each entry of a number, and pulled again to register the total.

Every transaction was sent to the office, whether paid for with cash or charged to an account. The receipt was sent to and from the office in a cylinder-shaped carrier that moved on a wire cable when pulled by a wooden handle.

I quit working in early 1950, because it was unacceptable that pregnant women work in public places!

MARY ANN LABUTTA

11

The War Years

The 1940's was a time when the entire country supported the war effort in both the European and the Pacific theaters.

Many products were strictly rationed, and many products were not available at all. Some rationed items were: meat, coffee, sugar, shortenings, tires, and gasoline. Each family (according to size) was issued ration books, and when one of the items was purchased, stamps from the ration books had to be turned in to the store. Even though gasoline and tires were rationed, anyone using these unnecessarily could be stopped, questioned and fined. My husband had to 'room' with a family near the school where he taught in 1941-1943, because he was not allowed tires and gasoline to travel 30 miles a day. Only those employed in a defense industry were permitted to drive that many miles.

The war years would be hard to imagine and compare to life as it is today. Important to remember: My parents' generation had large families, and common were those families with 4-8 children. When war was declared in December of 1941, there were many young men of 'draft age'. Many families had 2-4 sons who were drafted to serve our country wherever they were assigned. Three of my brothers (ages 25, 23, and 18) were drafted into the armed forces during the war years. Between 1942-1946 you would seldom see young men 18-35 years of age in our area. If so, they were fathers with two or more children, they were deferred for good reason, or they were in uniform and home 'on furlough'.

There was no manufacturing of cars, stoves, refrigerators, or any appliance. All manufacturing plants were converted to producing planes, ships, tanks, trucks, guns, and the many items needed to equip the armed forces. This change in manufacturing, coupled with the majority of young men called to serve our country, brought about the entrance of a large number of women into the plants and mills all over the country. "Rosie the Riveter" was a song about the women who worked in the manufacturing plants. Over the years, the entrance of so many women into the work force (who remained working outside the home), brought about a change in family life and even in our culture.

The only moving pictures we saw of what was happening overseas during the war, were the newsreels in the movie theaters. This was the time before the introduction of telephoto lens or television.

V-mail was the method used to send letters to service men overseas, and the way service men sent letters back to the States. V-mail was a one-sheet form for writing a letter on one side, and it folded into the size of a regular envelope. The V-mail were all sent via airmail, which was unusual at that time, because regular mail was sent by truck, train, or ship. Service men sent all their letters marked FREE in the corner of the envelope reserved for a postage stamp. Postage at that time cost 3 cents for regular mail, 6 cents for airmail, and 1 cent for a postcard.

When the war ended in Europe in May of 1945 and in the Pacific in August of 1945, it was several months before the manufacturing plants were converted to producing items for the civilian population. The demand for cars, stoves, refrigerators and appliances could not be met for at least a year. Customers names were put on a waiting list in a few retail stores, hoping their name would come to the top at one of the stores. We were married in the summer of 1946, and for six months I cooked on an electric hot plate and we used the refrigerator next door only when necessary. Then in early 1947, our name came to the top on a waiting list, and we were able to purchase both a stove and refrigerator——six months after we were married!

MARY ANN LABUTTA

12

Earlier Cars

Cars today have evolved from crude vehicles of the earlier years. My father carried an extra axle in the car (the 1920's), because the axle had a tendency to break easily. That may also have been caused by the many unpaved roads.

Several miles away, there was a 2-mile hill on U.S. Route 40. Men would take their cars to test whether the car could make it to the summit in high gear. Most cars had to be shifted to second gear, and even into low gear, before they reached the top of the mountainous hill. There was a 'watering trough' midway up this hill where the radiator of the car could be refilled——the majority of cars overheated on the drive up this long hill.

Cars had no sealed-beam headlights (even in the later decades), and those open bulbs would easily break. It was common to see cars with just one headlight. There was only one brake light on the back of the car, and turning signals were very far in the future. The driver had to extend the left arm out of the car window, and signal a left turn by pointing the index finger to the left. An upright thumb signaled a right turn. There were no backup lights. Can you imagine cars in todays traffic without those lights on the back of the car?

Windshield wipers worked somehow on a vacuum from the accelerator. The more you used the accelerator, the more the wipers would slow down to practically nothing——just when they were needed the most! In the winter months when the windshield was frozen, the driver would periodically get out of the car and manually scrape the ice and snow from the windshield. There were no defrosters, and when the first ones were put in cars, they were not efficient——no way to get heat to the windshield.

All cars were stick shift. Automatic transmissions were introduced in about 1940. There were no power brakes or power steering until long after World War II, so driving those cars was not at all like driving today. Flat tires were a common thing and the average life of a tire was 8,000-10,000 miles.

During the mid 1940's, I drove a 1935 Ford Roadster with a 'rumble seat' that was pulled up out of the back of the car. This convertible had a cloth top that was operated by hand. There were no roll-up windows. There were side curtains made of leather and isinglass (mica) that had to be snapped on. In the heat of summer driving with the curtains off, it would start to rain and I had to stop the car, snap on the curtains, then suffocate in the closed up car. The touring car that my father drove in the 1920's had the same type of curtains along the sides of the car.

These are some names of cars from yesteryear:

Cars from Yesteryear

La Salle	Studebaker
Packard	Austin/Healy
Elgin	Willys/Overland
Chandler	Nash
Stearns	Hudson

1923 Stearns

MARY ANN LABUTTA

EPILOGUE

Most telephones for home use were installed after World War II, and they were all on 'party' telephone lines. Three or more families were all on the same telephone line. You had to distinguish whether it was your call by the number of short rings—1, 2, 3 or 4 short rings. Sometimes you knew when a family on the same telephone line was deliberately eavesdropping on your conversation. This started to change in the late 1950's when private telephone lines were installed.

A few decades after World War II, everyday life was most influenced with the development of television, ballpoint pens, plastics and the interstate highways.

This personal account of life as experienced in the 1930's and 1940's, was written after many discussions with my husband. It is important to pass on these facts to the younger generations.

Hope these pages give some insight to what life was like years ago, and how very different it is today.

Made in the USA